The Butcher's Hands

For Jonathan, with love

Acknowledgements

Acknowledgements are due to the editors of the following
publications in which some of these poems first appeared:
*The Bread We Live By, The Frogmore Papers, Mslexia, The New
Writer, The North, The Piano on Fire, Reactions 3, The Rialto,
Smiths Knoll, Staple*

Thanks to Ros Barber and Jackie Wills for criticism, advice
and support.

Thanks also to The Authors' Foundation for an award in
2002 which enabled me to work on this book.

The Butcher's Hands

Catherine Smith

BLAG	MICK	P. TREE	ALLES	SPON	SINE
MOBILE	CHADD	NURSE	CENT	HOME	BIND
			3	05	

Smith/Doorstop Books

Published 2003 by
Smith/Doorstop Books
The Poetry Business
The Studio
Byram Arcade
Westgate
Huddersfield HD1 1ND

ISBN 1-902382-60-9

British Library Cataloguing-in-Publication Data. A
catalogue record for this book is available from the
British Library.

Typeset at The Poetry Business
Printed by Peepal Tree Press, Leeds
Cover design by Rob Macdonald
Author's photograph by Jonathan Smith

Distributed by Central Books Ltd, 99 Wallis Road,
London E9 5LN

The Poetry Business gratefully acknowledges the help
of Arts Council England and Kirklees Cultural
Services.

CONTENTS

The Butcher's Hands

A stripped sheep
sags on its hook
behind the butcher.

This one's new.
A pale, eager boy
in a smoothed apron;

hands freshly scrubbed,
nails bitten to the quick.
He's learning the patter,

recommends lamb chops
and grips the knife; cuts
precisely between ribs,

then both hands on the hacksaw –
I watch his bird-bone wrists,
his muscle and sinew,

his blood and meat
beneath the skin.
One slip, and he'll spill open.

Twenty years on, he'll be
a family man with three prime kids,
their photos over the till;

his knuckles shining,
palms red as mutton,
the tip of one finger, missing.

Gravid

The first time was on the Northern Line,
a hot, airless evening, reeking of latex
and aftershave, bodies pressed
in a reluctant multiple confinement.
She got on at Cockfosters, sullen and pale;
I tried not to stare but the swell of her belly –
couldn't tear my eyes from the landscape
of stretched skin straining under the thin
cotton of her dress. One touch,
a quiet cupping of that hard, hot shape;
her scream ripped my ears.
The other passengers tutted, sank back
into their *Evening Standards.*

Much easier, after that; there are places
where they go. The hospital lift,
on the way up to Maternity,
clots of them bulged together
too busy breathing and counting
to notice a grey man clutching dahlias –
a tiny movement as the mechanism jolted,
a muttered apology. In that state
they fill so much space – greedy
with flesh and breath – and the groaning,
the hand in the small of the back, pushing
further towards me – I'd have been a fool
not to take advantage.

These days I'm in control;
there's one I pay. Eight months gone
and tight as a drum – sometimes I think
she'll split. She swaggers in,
with lycra stretched above the hump

her umbilicus like a beige cherry
stuck on for laughs, belly branded by
the track of her linea nigra.
She lets me feel, from breast to pubis,
the jerks and punches under the skin;
she calls it the little bastard. Sometimes
she lets me lick the length of it; I tell her
I think he likes this. He's turning.

Uncle Aubrey

Uncle Aubrey is dying. On the line
pummelled by freezing winds
nightclothes bluster and bulge.

Talk to him, cheer him up, says Olwyn
so I tell him I have walked on the moor
and seen hawks hunting mice.

Hands pared to bone, he twists fingers
and remembers dead cousins
dead drunk at Christmas.

His head is too heavy for his neck,
and his eyes are too clotted
to take me in.

He is dying in Welsh. It is part of me
singing somewhere in my blood
voices of sickness and rain.

Detritus

She starts with a cupboard, ditching skirts
and dresses which no longer fit or suit. The lace top
she wore to Andrea's wedding which confirmed
her lack of cleavage; out it goes. The bin bag
crackles in her hands. Its weight makes her gasp
and she ties a knot in the top and tells herself

she'll stop, in a moment. Once she's searched
under her son's unmade bed, and excavated
three ten-franc coins filmed with dust,
a headless green one-legged Power Ranger,
a stegosaurus with a bitten tail, a book token
from last Christmas and the plastic wristband

he wore the day he was born, the one he asked for
and promised to keep safe. She sits back,
reads his name, his sex, his weight in kilos,
meaningless. Thinks of marbled breasts, the weight
of them outrageous, the sting of gummed nipples.
The way her milk wasn't white, but thin and blue.

Vigil

Midnight. A cool draught across his face, a dent
in their mattress. His wife's on the landing,
the hem of her nightdress brushing her ankles,

her fingertips outstretched towards the GI
who taught her to jitterbug and French kiss,
who took her virginity in her mother's front room.

She's twenty again. Her breath smells of tobacco,
not Horlicks and TCP. The backs of her knees
prickle in new nylons. She's laughing,

head flung back, throat white and taut,
lips slicked. She keeps perfect time.
No trace of stiffness in vigorous arms

and she swings him round, high on gin
and the Squadronnaires. She slows, freezes,
a living statue. The music dies.

Her skin's translucent, liver spotted, now
her lover's gone. Paper eyelids; her stalk neck
slackens onto his chest. They sway together

at the top of the stairs and in the moonlight
patches of her scalp gleam pink.
One slip and they could fall. He guides her

back to bed, folds her arms across
wasted breasts. Tomorrow she'll ask
what his name is, whether it's time to dance.

Keepsakes

Each time it's something, slipped inside her bag. At first
she keeps it simple – a marble from the solitaire board,
the innards of his pen, a sock, yellowed with sweat.

One night she hears him singing in the bath, and removes
used plasters from the heels of his trainers. She pats him dry
when he's done, sucks water from the wet snakes of his hair,

and rubs his shoulders. When he takes a girl's call in bed
she slips into his study, removes the polished alabaster egg
that weights their numbers to his desk.

When she returns he's sleeping, the white sheets
stained and creased. Going through his bin
she finds fresh toenail clippings and receipts for flowers.

She dresses to the slow beat of his breathing. At home,
she empties out her bag and shapes him on her bed –
flower receipt eyes, sock prick, alabaster heart.

Personae

Today Mrs. West is being Queen Victoria.
Shoulders banked regally on plumped pillows,
she offers her fingers for Dr. Leighton's kiss.

Yesterday she was Cleopatra, breasts bared;
blacked round her eyes with felt-pens
she'd pinched from Occupational Therapy.

Her Mata Hari phase was tricky; she flashed
her belly at Mr. Jones from the League of Friends,
who has a pacemaker. He had to lie down.

Tomorrow we're hoping for the Virgin Mary;
she's always placid for the Angel Gabriel.
I am blessed, she says, and keeps her nightie on.

Hen Night

By her fifth Bacardi Breezer, she's sweating cobs,
her L-plates have come askew and her make-up's
gothic. The stripper's a big disappointment;

puts his back out giving her a fireman's lift
and ignores her mate asking to squeeze his hose.
By midnight her guts are growling

and, crouched by the bog in The King's Head,
wave after wave of rice and peas
leaping like salmon into the bowl, her head pounds,

it hurts to breathe, and she knows
when the ring slides over her knuckle, there'll be
this sour taste, still, this bruising on her knees.

Waiting For The Foot-Binder

The last evening of toes. She flexes them
so they splay in the dust like stunted fans.

Dusk thickens over the village. Chickens
worry the dirt with their staccato beaks;

she chases them with her younger brother.
He laughs. He is too fast for her.

Tomorrow the foot-binder will sing as she
holds her down, and folds each foot into a fist.

Snow

You stand outside on a day when the sky's
thick and silent with snow, when each flake
drifts down to whiten the landscape
and you open your mouth. The first
flakes land on your tongue and teeth
like tissue, before melting, but gradually
your throat fills, the snow packs tight,
your guts turn solid and blue. Your blood
carries its own icebergs. Your eyes
shut tight under their layers of ice, your ears
full of the sound of your own winter –
the creak and shift, the slow bang of your heart.

Infestation

You hear them before you see or smell them –
their bald feet pattering under floorboards.
You listen for sudden thumps, muted squeaks,
knowing they're growing fat on crumbs
they've foraged. Your crumbs. Think of them
sleeking their fur with sandpaper tongues.
You know they're breeding down there –
the females swelling in the dark, like bread,
and imagine them curled asleep together,
all those bodies in one soft, breathing ball,
their babies naked and blind,
while the house ticks on above them.
You open a cupboard and find
their tiny black shits, the stench of their piss –
through a hole you spot a brown face,
luminous eyes. You know, then,
they're laughing at you, they've taken over –
and you sweat, believing
they're chewing through wires,
that your house will burn down in the night,
the smoke will fill your throat before you wake,
you'll be found too late, blackened to a crisp,
and tell yourself, as you lay down poison,
they won't feel pain, after all,
it's not as if they're human,
and there are so many of them,
with their dirt, a few less is a blessing,
and you sleep better, knowing the bodies
will rot quietly, out of sight.

Hover

Over the runway, the Fairey Swordfish hovers,
the pilot shrunk to a dot. Propellers
churn the heat, sting our ears.

It stays up there by some collective will,
and if we stare long enough
the engine won't sputter into silence,

we won't freeze, like extras in a wartime film,
as it unravels through slow seconds,
lurching towards us. We won't

gather our kids, cover their heads
as the fuselage splits open,
sends fire singing through the crowd,

whose skin chars, peels and flutters off,
like papers on fortune cookies.
These things won't happen. The Swordfish

will stay suspended in the present.
Its shadow will darken each of us
for a moment, and we will keep it

far enough above us
so the pilot remains a god,
his engine running, his face invisible.

Boy Child

Grandma's hands are masked with flour
and she's letting me sprinkle sugar on the plums
when she looks up, points to the ceiling.
My baby,
she says, flattening pastry,
my airing cupboard baby. Funny.
He hardly ever cries.

Her fifth, she explains, a boy child,
(a secret baby,
no-one else knows) –
a black-haired boy, good as gold.
She keeps him under the towels
and the spare electric blanket.

Can we take him out? I ask,
what does he eat? What does he like?
She smiles, shrugs,
drapes a pastry sheet over the fruit.
He likes what I like. Iced Gems, the pink ones.
He likes the dark.

I press my cheek to her belly.
We'll get him later, she says,
pushing me away, *when the pie's ready.*
I imagine him snug on her hip
as she knifes the crust, their faces
glowing in the burst of steam.

Feeding On Demand

Today he's pale and sullen,
spooning ice-cream between lips that frame
adult teeth in a boy's mouth. He grunts when I ask

Are you enjoying it? This is our treat, a cold
café in an unfamiliar high street, five minutes
from the school where he knows no one

and no one knows how, once, I was the meal,
my flat brown nipple sore in his fierce mouth
as he frowned up at me, milking me dry.

Monopoly

Almost bankrupt and only recently released from jail,
she owes her ten year old
four hundred quid in rent
for landing on his new hotel in Bond Street.
He owns most of the West End
and several public utilities.
She pleads poverty. He points out
she could give him Leicester Square
and they could come to some arrangement
over her arrears. She thinks how

this is what capitalism does to children,
– brutalises them, makes them worship
five-hundred pound notes, little red boxes,
encourages them to sniff out the weak
and charge them exorbitant rent,
rob them blind, make them beg.
She watches his fingers fatten on his stash

and she tells him, no. She'll take her chances,
and hangs onto Leicester Square. She likes
the Japanese men with their cameras,
their perfect hair, their busy hands,
she likes the pigeon shit, the café
with the gilt-framed photo of the Queen
where the waiter gives her extra chocolate
on her cappuccino, no favours asked.

Reunion, Zennor Coastal Path

Mist dissolves St Ives, somewhere in the distance.
This is the path we walked fifteen years ago,
newly married, after our night of hotel sex,
our full English breakfast. We see our younger selves
coming towards us – you with your map and Doc Martens,
your thick, brown hair, me following in my red cagoule,
my hair dyed gothic-black, my unlined skin.
We could be planning an argument or a long kiss.
We're silent and our faces, hard to read in the damp air,
give nothing away. We think how volatile we were then,
smile indulgently, let ourselves pass, when we see
the momentary smirk on our younger faces
as we struggle, for a moment, to catch our breath.

Australia

We reached the earth's core by lunch time.
Blistering molten rock, spewing upwards,

and heat that seared eyeballs and lips.
More digging, and by mid-afternoon,

sweating, we knew we'd arrived.
Light dazzled us; we knew the meek

bleating of sheep, the shock of scorched air.
You promised me the first kangaroo;

like a brown dog, you said, only bigger, and I
could ride in its pouch drinking Kia-Ora,

and you'd throw boomerangs which would
flash like fish, and in Australia you must

keep walking or running or you'll spiral
off the surface of the earth. You can crunch

red ants, sweet and gritty as sugar.
No one makes you eat beetroot or mince.

By tea-time, they drew the curtains on the room
where you lay, mouth open, not talking,

and only I knew where you were; thousands
of miles away, with your voice upside-down.

Statement

I did not take the last of the milk; someone else
spilled red wine over the crossword and
I'm proud to say I've never hit my children.

I wasn't there when the car got scratched.
I never once cheated in a spelling test, never
felt tempted to try a same-sex relationship.

Chopin moves me to tears. I eat green vegetables
for the joy of it. Everything in my shopping bag
I've paid for with my own, hard-earned cash.

A clear conscience is a wonderful comfort.
These are not tears, but drops of glycerine –
a gift from the alien who dead-heads my roses.

Breathe

Thirteen floors up, the air is thinner, comes in canisters
and tastes metallic. Faces loom. *Breathe. Breathe.*

I'm sucking in, sucking the whole white world into my lungs,
I'm beached and floundering on the wet red sheets –

I'm splitting open like a whale when they reach in
with the chainsaws. Drowning in air. *Breathe. Breathe.*

You fucking breathe, smug bitch. I breathe enough to last
a lifetime, a lung-time of blue breath. A clenched face

bats my thigh; shoulders and body, hauled into the light.
Silence. Then a damp engine, spluttering into life.

Acoustic

Now the small room is stripped,
three layers of wallpaper scraped clear,
outlines of light switches
pale under flaking paint,
the old carpet sagging in the skip,
a baby's cry
seeps through the walls.
It's there all the time,
leaking between floorboards,
a thin white sound
souring her saliva,
robbing her of sleep.
She waits for the plasterer
to cover the cracked walls,
for new carpet to seal it up,
but it rings like tinnitus.
Something tells her it's a girl,
hungry for milk.

Kingfisher

You split the frozen water with your boot,
disturb the shuttlecock of green and blue
lodged in the black. Under a mercury sky
we ask ourselves; did it freeze down there,
excited by a flickering fish, did it
swoop, pierce the surface, drown?

You toe it over, and its chestnut belly,
its lucent greens and blues smash home
like the icy shock of drowning.
I remember when we
coloured up for love.

These days we're drab, polite, though
nothing changes the freckles on your belly,
the piston of your throat,
the way you unpeel fruit.

The sky tears, peppers us
with freezing rain. We take shelter,
sucking our fingertips back to life, ignoring
the iridescent flash at our feet.

Stornoway Harbour

This is the sea of your childhood, diesel-thick,
slapping Styrofoam from the burger bar
against the sides of blue and orange boats.

On the quay, mackerel convulse in buckets,
grinning like madmen; a rictus of scales,
salt-stink. The smell shifts in my stomach.

In the bay seals, heads gravestone-grey,
nose the black water. *They're always there*
you say, and together we watch the men

toss writhing arcs of petrol-blue and slate.
Serene, they duck and surface. They'll wait
forever; Gods, with the patience of stone.

Night Bus

I know where you are.
You're on the night bus,
lit-up like an aquarium
in the dark, your face
pressed against the glass.
You float along the coast road,
past the slumped pier,
the padlocked beach-huts,
and you're the only passenger –
just you and the driver
the last men awake,
like dry, twitching fish
while the city sleeps,
its eyes stitched tight
against the black.

Formica

Leicester Forest West, between coaches.
In the café, the formica reads *Jason fucked Gemma.*

Sipping bitter tea, I wonder if the striplights
fizzed for a moment when he switched them off,

whether he went on top, whether the sharp arc
of the table sliced her back, whether

iridescent grains of sugar pressed into her flesh,
whether she got up stiffly, shaking out her hair,

stood in the drizzle waiting for the Manchester bus,
while he took out his penknife and began carving.

Wonders

(Julia Pastrana, a bearded woman, was billed as 'the ugliest woman in the world', by her 'manager', Mr Lent. The couple later married.)

The earth is cooling now. All day they've sweated
in the August heat, his Wonders,
twenty seven rescued freaks. Prodded
by ignorant children, they've proffered
limbs and faces, caused women to faint.
Only he sees their beauty, the human template
twisted by Satan or God.

He tends them carefully, his strange flock,
bidding them good-night by name –
Angus the Lobster Boy, Pedro the Wart-Man.
His dog barks as he tucks up Martha and Mary,
twitching their shared hip. He checks the locks
on the caravans, as the stars burn
above the French village, miles from civilisation.

And Julia waits patiently at their polished table.
She's lowered the lamps,
brushed and oiled her beard, the way he likes.
Tonight they'll play cribbage into the early hours,
he'll smoke three cheroots, she'll chide him
in her tiny voice. He'll unbutton her,
lay her flat, sleep deeply on her hair-shirt skin.

The New Bride

Dying, darling, is the easy bit. Fifty paracetamol,
bride-white and sticking in the throat, ten shots
of Johnny Walker, and the deed is done.
A twilight day of drowsing, then the breathing
slows to a whisper, like a sinner in Confession.

Death is dead easy. No, what happens next
is the difficulty. You bastard, howling in public,
snivelling over photos, ringing round for consolation.
And you have me burnt, like a dinner gone wrong,
you keep the charred remains of me on show

at the Wake, inviting everyone I hate. Oh God,
they come in packs, sleek as rats with platitudes
and an eye on my half of the bed, hoping to find
leftover skin, a hint of fetid breath. I leave them
no hairs on the pillow; there are none to leave.

And a year to the day since I shrug off the yoke
of life, you meet the new bride. In group therapy.
You head straight for a weeper and wailer,
telling strangers all her little tragedies. You love
the way she languishes, her tears sliming your neck,

you give into her on vile pink Austrian blinds.
The Wedding is a riot of white nylon. Everybody
drinks your health and hers, the simpering bitch.
She and Delia Smith keep you fat and happy
as a pig in shit. I want her cells to go beserk.

Some nights I slip between you. The new bride
sleeps buttoned up, slug-smug in polyester. You,

my faithless husband, turn over in your dreams,
and I'm there, ice-cold and seeking out your eyes
and for a moment you brush my lips, and freeze.

Bad Fairy

I'm icing summer. Your prize roses
curl and die, birds freeze, mid flight,

rain down onto compost heaps, bounce
off your house, your car. Now you'll see

crops whiten under brilliant skies,
lambs turn to cardboard on the hills,

your children, in their thin clothes,
will find their lips and fingers turning blue,

and it's too late to say you're sorry,
keep your promises, send me back.

Reconstruction

Four twenty-two pm. The sky darkens above the swings. A
man loads film. You knot a tie around your neck, slick
Vaseline across your lips, buckle yourself into navy gabar-
dine, a wet-hair smell seeped in the fibres. You're aware of a
hem, unravelling. The violin case bangs against your legs
and the shoes skin your heels, but it's for a good cause, and
the policewoman whispers reassurance, tells you to speed up
past the launderette where the local boys chew gum, drum
their heels on the dryers, watch you. Four twenty-nine, you
pass Leonie Shearer's Stage School. Through blazing windows you see dancers, pink sugar mice, toes correctly
pointed. A brown dog runs up, slimes your palm, quivers its
nose into your crotch and you hesitate, then sidestep, you
keep your head down, leaving the High-Street smell of car
fumes and kebabs as you join the path, and that's when your
belly drops thirty floors without warning because there's no
camera now, no voice in your ear, just the black water in the
puddle underfoot, the buddleia with its burnt-torch flowers,
rustling. The London train throbs past, you see the station
lights ahead, you tell yourself, keep calm, you tell yourself,
this is not happening, these footsteps biting your heels, the
cold thump of your blood. Four thirty-six, the darkness
wraps you, his breath mists your ear, he only wants to talk.
His fingers smell of Pears' soap. He calls you someone else's
name, unbuttons you carefully. You're a gift.

Poecilia Reticulata

All week you trust me with their fragile food,
brittle fragments stinking of old salt.

I pepper the surface of their world
and they thrust upwards, lips flexing,

avoiding my eyes. Sometimes I tap the glass
and they scatter, like balls of mercury.

Sometimes I press my face up close
and mouth silent insults.

They flit disdainfully through arches and castles
as I run my fingers over forbidden surfaces –

mantelpiece, paperweight, books. I study
your desk diary. A clean, assertive script,

an ordered life, with good beech floors
and iridescent fish. My wrist slips.

On the last day, they rise
and bob like litter in the cackling water.

Fellatio

is a type of pasta. Best bought fresh,
not the dried stuff shelved
between Home Baking and Biscuits.

Enjoy *fellatio Vongole*,
packed with clams, salty and tight
as miniature vaginas. Alternatively,

try it *al Funghi*, the mushrooms
earthy under the tongue, or
al Pomodoro (healthy, low fat).

Serve naked, in candlelight.
Part your lips. Don't rush.
Savour every mouthful.

Absolute

Nothing is absolute. Even thick snow
stifling roof-tops and roads, can't silence
the suggestion of wind in the distance.

Even solid ice sealing a winter pond,
tight as a lid, splits under the strain
of one too many pairs of skates.

Even when you pledged absolute love
you kept her letters, all of them,
in blue tissue, in a bottom drawer.

Pastoral

My dog has rounded up a lamb, left it
buckled, shaking on damp grass.
It sags like a carpet bag as I stagger
round the field, looking for its mother.

Dagged yellow wool, knotted
as an unwashed beard. Its tongue
droops, like a scrap of pink balloon.
Each weak bleat reminds me

I'm crap at dogs, this country lark.
The sky blackens; I imagine
the lamb's heart stuttering to a stop,
the burden solid in my arms.

In the distance, a clot of sheep glares.
I lower it by a hedge. Its piss
steams in the cold air, the smell
of wet wool soiling my fleece, my hands.

Calculation

The mathematics of drops
is a delicate matter.
I measure him, note his weight

to the nearest pound.
Thirteen stones, seven.
A drop of eight feet, two inches.

His skin's smooth
with fine musculature of the throat.
A small vein, jumping.

We're face to face.
His green eyes,
a cracked front tooth.

On the day, I enter the cell quietly
at exactly three minutes
before the appointed time,

pass the body-belt around his waist,
pinion his arms, the leather
tight against his shirt.

The buckles click fast,
and the Priest mumbles, as if
his God could help anybody now –

only the certainty of Italian hemp rope,
finest quality – pliable, strong –
ensures complete dislocation

of the atlas and axis.
The white sack fills
with my man's breathing.

I adjust the ring
behind his left ear, just so,
place him under the beam,

pinion his legs beneath the knees.
I whisper to him
he's in good hands.

Resurrection

You might crash into the window
like a sudden ragged moth, banging
against the bright glass, or worse,

you'll appear in my mirror, leering
over one shoulder, yellow-skinned,
and bury your fingers in my hair,

or worse still, you'll slouch by my trolley
at the cold meats counter, whisky-foul
and lewd, chewing pastrami. I know

you'll reconstitute head and heart
and lungs and liver and limbs, emerge
from that grey ash, solidify yourself,

breathe into my face. I dream about
the hot grip of your fingers, the dry rasp
of your voice – *listen, it is not finished.*

Soul

The Presbyterian on my doorstep tells me
my lack of religious conviction means
I'm an unfit mother to my innocent children,
my soul is currently in the possession of Lucifer.

I decide my soul is a small brown dog
(of interest only to me and Lucifer),
an ugly mongrel (part terrier), with a penchant
for wine gums and shagging strangers' ankles,

and it grew savage and grizzled –
incontinent and snappy, one ear
frilled by fighting, a rheumy left eye.
A liability, its breath stinking of old meat.

So I tell the Presbyterian Lucifer's welcome to it.

The Amputees' Race

(Amputees from the First World War, convalescing at Alder Hey Hospital, were filmed taking part in a Sports Day).

They're off, twelve men,
each with one trouser leg

pinned, neat as a tent flap,
lunging forward on crutches

faces blurred,
a clean white napkin

tied around each neck.
The camera pans to the crowd

roaring them on,
and when they reach the finish

they're greeted by a row of apples
dangling on strings.

Officers clap, cajole
as each man lifts his face

towards the swinging fruit,
mouths gape, bite and

bite at the flesh, juice
running down chins.

The film loops. They jerk
back to the beginning, race again.

The Smoking Room

I dream you've died.
Doctors slit you open,
boil meat from bone.

They wire your skeleton
and hang you from a pole,
a hook through your skull.

Your hips jangle.
They take you to their smoking room,
your grin amuses them.

They smoke cheroots, pipes, fat cigars.
The room fogs up,
ceiling brown as old teeth.

Your bones take on
the patina of their habit,
while their own lungs blacken.

One night I rescue you,
climb through the window,
breathe the stink they've left,

unhook you tenderly.
Fold you in my arms,
run and run,

your bones warming
against my skin.

What She Sees

She's sent outside while they unpack. *Go and see.*
First she sees the lizard, its back patterned like carpet,
belly pulsing faster than her breath. She sees it shoot
into a crack, swallowed by dark. Next she sees plums,

blue as day-old bruises, accepting her thumbprint,
their orange flesh slashed open by a heel. Face down
and silent in the scorched grass she watches bees
bristling the lavender to a frenzy. Dry, sullen heat

prickles at her neck and knees; she tracks a beetle
on the path, listens to the splashes and echoes
from a neighbour's pool. She sees her father's face
at a window, the sharp planes of cheek and bone

white from his indoor life. She sees him vanish.
She runs into the sudden cool of dry flagstones
and sees a puddle of clothes by a bed, pale limbs
knotted hard and hot, sudden lights behind her eyes.

Revelation

She finds the changing room
when no-one's looking.
First her clothes, then
a lateral slit. Her skin comes off
in seconds, one firm tug,

gives itself up
cleanly, without reproach,
lies draped like a parachute
around her feet,
a thin, translucent thing.

She hangs it from a peg
marvelling at how light
she feels, how free,
how good it is to shed
what isn't needed –

the crows' feet, sun spots,
frown lines, years spent
half-alive, grief
dulling her skin,
splitting her lips.

Stripped, it's a joy
to see her veins,
fast and blue,
the harp-string muscles,
even the yellowed fat.

The mirror gives back
the fist-shaped womb
with her stone daughters,
thirty this month,
snug in their flesh cave.

Last Orders

Dispose of feathers from the bedroom carpet.
Shave your head carefully,

watch your skull emerge in the mirror
your beautiful, forgotten skull.

Wearing the cotton gloves provided
carefully clean and polish all surfaces.

Cut yourself out of family photographs
Wipe your voice from the answering machine.

Split the last of the Sycamore.
Pile logs neatly in the wood shed.

Ignore the splinter
embedded in your right thumb.

Enter the waiting room in silence,
through the red door.

Take a seat. Avoid eye contact
with the woman opposite.

At the last minute you will remember
the smell of creosote,

that time the wall-eyed goat
suckled your elbow.

When the loud speakers call your name,
you will go at once.

Charades

Strangle Bully Delicious, you whisper in my ear.
Pretend it's a film. Go on. I throttle my own throat,
kick out. I mime guzzling ice-cream, dripping

with desire. You're making me grotesque, a freak
with bulging neck, gobstopper eyes,
lashing the audience while licking my lips;

they call out *Gladiator, The Nutty Professor,*
Frankenstein, Nine and a Half Weeks.
You cackle as my movements grow more frantic.

No-one guesses. *Tell us.* You hug me tight,
and our guilty secret hums like radiation
between us. Strangle. Bully. Delicious.

Picture This

You come into focus most clearly on windy Mondays,
Grandad's shirt sleeves applauding on the line,
curtains boiling at windows. Your cheeks, normally pale,

slapped red by sudden gusts; I see you bending,
stiff-backed, to retrieve a peg or yank a dandelion,
then your apron snarls itself up and your dress

lifts sharply to reveal the tops of stockings pinching
mottled thighs. I can hold you there for several seconds
until your hair escapes its pins and leaves you blurred.

Trick

The Ocelot coat in the cupboard; still there,
mints in the inside pocket. His wife's best,
worn only to High Mass and Whitley Bay.

It used to sashay round her hips,
so sleek and mobile it almost purred.
Creaking now, a corpse on its hanger.

He waits for her head to sprout from the collar,
her mouth to move in the mothballed dark,
two pointed fingers to shoot from the left cuff,

bang bang bang, that got you;
now do that trick you always did
with the insides of your trouser pockets.
The one about the baby elephant.

Feathers

Afterwards, they roll apart,
thumbprints fading on her breasts.
They dream. She dreams
she's naked in a park,
sun prickling her shoulders,
scattering grain for peacocks
whose beaks sip at the lawn,
blue throats smooth as glass,
trailed feathers limp as tail-coats;
he dreams he looks up,
sees her quiet skin,
the deft, methodical wrists
and he stops feeding,
draws himself tall,
his feathers rattle
open and up, a hundred
staring turquoise eyes,
each one a signature, a *yes.*

Cast

Safeways, Wednesday morning,
and the tannoy cracks like a knuckle:

James Dean, please go to fresh fruit and veg.
I can't believe I'm hearing this,

I'm standing there,
imagining James Dean

under the strident lights
scratch his arse

as he unpacks carrots.
And then I'm thinking –

Oliver Reed in wines and spirits,
polishing bottles of Remy Martin

on his uniform sleeve,
careful as a midwife.

Bette Davis,
muttering to herself,

arranging bottles of bleach
in the household products aisle,

Alfred Hitchcock
collecting trolleys in the car park

herding them quietly
in the thin September rain,

Marilyn Monroe
on the far checkout,

blonde as ice-cream,
packing beef and onion pies for a pensioner.

I wonder what they talk about
in the staff room –

if they're in the Christmas Club
and moan about the store manager –

and then I stop daydreaming and stare,
as Marlon Brando leans into the chiller cabinet

to stack blocks of unsalted butter
with keen, precise hands.

The Real McCoy

Four floors up, the air is thinner. When I see one
toss her hair, arch her throat, I can scarcely breathe.

Summertime is best, when the heat wraps them up
like luscious parcels. Some are barely dressed.

At night I head for the bar with no mirrors and wait.
I choose a quiet one. Her skin has ripened in the sun

and her neck tastes of vanilla under my tongue.
I fill her full of Bloody Marys and compliments.

We sway home past the Pier, lit up like an X-ray.
There's salt in her hair as my key crunches in the lock.

She wants to know my name. *McCoy,* I tell her.
You're freezing, she complains. *Your fingers are like ice.*

She's drowsy at the end; the spurt of red exhausts her.
I'm cold, she says. I'm too busy drinking to reply.

Lunch

Gina sips her cappuccino, makes a list
with Mrs. Farrell's fountain pen
in Mrs. Farrell's velvet notebook.
Pair of sea-horses, and tank.
Nipples and/or labia pierced.
Oyster silk matching bra
and thong. Champagne at the Grand,
graffiti in ladies' toilet. Cigar.
Mrs. Farrell's mink drags at Gina's shoulders.
She splays a set of credit cards
like a good hand at poker. She'll start
directly. A spree in Knickerbox,
then a long lunch in that place
Mrs. Farrell talks about. Exclusive,
stiff white tablecloths, silver cutlery
gleaming, waiters with manicured nails.
She thinks how Mrs. Farrell's fat
from too many lunches, from too many
afternoons sipping gin slings
with her fat smug friends on their fat
smug arses. Now Mrs. Farrell's gagged,
trussed up on her pink bedspread, unfed
since last night. Gina's stomach growls.

Feral

Our new exhibit. Approximately
thirteen years, small, but fully developed.
Nostrils flared, otherwise
recognisably human. As you see
she's naked, scrawny, covered in a soft
downy hair. Defecates freely.
See how her hands clutch her knees
as she rocks. Listen. A muted,
whimpering howl. Dislikes us
banging on the glass, bares her teeth.
Sleeps curled, like a dog.
We hope to civilise her in time,
but she's resisted our attempts
to stroke or clothe her. She's a biter,
this one. She draws blood.
She feeds twice a day, she likes
her meat raw. See the way
she spits out gristle, the way
she gnaws on bone. Look at how
her eyes glitter as she stares.

Marcus

I found him in a skip, head and torso down, long limbs
pink and hairless. Three hard tugs and he was mine.
He had to be laid flat in the back of the car
but didn't criticise my driving. I sang

all the way home, bathed him and rubbed him dry,
patted and stroked his fabulous glazed hump.
He never stopped smiling as I chewed his ears
and scraped his belly with my greedy teeth.

He tasted of fresh plastic, with a hint of Badedas.
I gave up Tai Chi, cancelled my Counsellor,
rang into work with faked complaints. We embraced,
watched daytime telly with the curtains drawn.

He didn't despise the fat or bald, never bitched
about Richard and Judy, or moaned about my drinking,
my chocolate cravings, my spitting cherry stones.
I loved the way he never sighed or snarled or spoke …

It's been three days. He's even better candle-lit.
I drizzle champagne on his chest as shadows jump.
Here's to us, Marcus. I lick his pristine skin,
and kiss his silent, rigid lips.

Postulant

The morning of her vows to Christ
Sister Patricia cracks a fertilized egg.
The chick's eyes are sealed tight,
head huge on its wizened body,
bright blood filming the yolk.

Later, scissors, then a razor,
are wielded over her scalp,
leaving it coarse as a man's chin.
Her nape prickles in a draught.
Palms pressed, she kneels

and raises her eyes to the crucifix.
Today she'll be His bride,
shaved clean, a vessel for His will,
leached of desire. Metal
floods her saliva; she imagines

the chick's eyelids split open,
wings itching free, heaving itself
from the smashed shell,
its naked skull
bearing the dent of her spoon.